LivHOME®

Live long. Live well. LivHOME.™

On behalf of the LivHOME team, I would
like to take this opportunity to thank you for
allowing us to serve your needs.

As a token of our appreciation,
we hope you enjoy this short book.

We will continue to provide you with the
highest level of service across all aspects
of our relationship with you.

TO

_____

FROM

_____

Published by Simple Truths
1952 McDowell Road, Suite 205
Naperville, IL 60563-65044

Design: Rich Nickel

Photos:
Nels Akerlund *(www.nelsakerlund.com):* pages 150, 154
Joe Decker: page 142
Bruce Heinemann *(www.theartofnature.com):* pages 22, 24, 30, 34, 36, 66, 70, 72, 100, 102, 106, 114, 118, 124, 130, 138, 156
Ken Jenkins *(www.kenjenkins.com):* pages 6, 60, 148
Rich Nickel *(www.richnickeldesign.com):* cover, page 58
Todd Reed *(www.toddreedphoto.com):* pages 42, 82, 112
Steve Terrill *(www.terrillphoto.com):* pages 10, 18, 28, 40, 46, 52, 54, 64, 78, 84, 90, 96, 144
Jeff Vanuga *(www.jeffvanugaphotography.com):* pages 88, 120

Printed and bound in China

ISBN: 978-1-60810-025-5

www.simpletruths.com
(800) 900-3427

01 4CPG 09

finding joy

Simple Secrets to a Happy Life

by Mac Anderson

simple truths®
THE GIFT OF INSPIRATION

www.simpletruths.com

Introduction
By Mac Anderson

Life can be complicated, but happiness…is simple. Of course, we try our best to make it complicated, but if we look closely, it's really very simple. And that's what this little book is all about…Simple Secrets to a Happy Life!

My goal is to have you sit down in a quiet place, and to slowly soak up every simple page. Don't hurry, just take a deep breath, read each thought, and reflect on how it might apply to your life. Think about what is…and what could be, if your mind and heart is open to change.

But here is the real key to making this book all it can be…*keep it close, and read it often.* Because in a perfect world we read something once, record it in our brain, and never need to read it again.

Well, I don't know about you, but my world is far from perfect. I have doubts, fears and disappointments in my life, and I need doses of inspiration to bring me back to where I should be…to re-direct me to what's really important in life. And this little book, if you'll let it, can be *that source of inspiration!* In just a few minutes it can put a smile on your face, and in your heart when you need it most.

My sincere hope is that you will use it…make it a constant source of inspiration. And just one more thing…share it with those you love!

Here's to life ~

Mac Anderson
Founder; Simple Truths

*I*t is one of the most beautiful
compensations in life…that no man
can sincerely try to help another
without helping himself.

RALPH WALDO EMERSON

The most important things in life aren't things.

ANTHONY D'ANGELO

Forgiveness does not change the past,

but it does enlarge the future.

PAUL BOESE

*K*nowledge is like
climbing a mountain.
The higher you reach the more
you can see and appreciate.

———

UNKNOWN

The quality of a person's life is in direct proportion to their commitment to excellence, regardless of their chosen field of endeavor.

VINCE LOMBARDI

Sometimes the best helping hand you can get is a good, firm push.

———

JOANN THOMAS

Joy is not in things;

it is in us.

RICHARD WAGNER

*I*f you don't stand for something,

you'll fall for anything.

———

UNKNOWN

Change always comes
bearing gifts.

———

PRICE PRITCHETT

*Kindness is the language
which the deaf can hear
and the blind can see.*

———

MARK TWAIN

*I*magination is the highest kite one can fly.

LAUREN BACALL

Far away there in the sunshine
are my highest aspirations.
I may not reach them, but I can look up
and see their beauty, believe in them,
and try to follow where they lead.

———

LOUISA MAY ALCOTT

finding joy

Create the highest, grandest
vision for your life because
you become what you believe.

———

OPRAH WINFREY

Whether you think you can,

or think you can't...

you're right.

HENRY FORD

He is rich or poor

according to what he is,

not according to what he has.

HENRY WARD BEECHER

*C*hange your thoughts and change your world.

———

NORMAN VINCENT PEALE

From small beginnings
come great things.

———

PROVERB

Service is the rent we pay to be living. It is the very purpose of life and not something you do in your spare time.

MARION EDELMAN

*U*nless you try to do something

beyond what you have already mastered,

you will never grow.

RALPH WALDO EMERSON

*The true meaning of life
is to plant trees under whose shade
you do not expect to sit.*

NELSON HENDERSON

*Y*our future depends
on many things,
but mostly yourself.

———

FRANK TYGER

Inch by inch, life's a cinch.

Yard by yard life is hard.

———

UNKNOWN

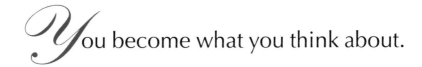

You become what you think about.

EARL NIGHTINGALE

Courage does not always roar.

Sometimes it is a quiet voice at the end of the day,

saying…"I will try again tomorrow."

———

MARY ANNE RADMACHER

A quiet conscience
sleeps in thunder.

———

ENGLISH PROVERB

When you learn, teach.

When you get, give.

———

MAYA ANGELOU

*L*et us always meet each other with a smile, for the smile is the beginning of love.

MOTHER TERESA

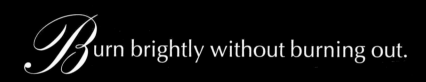

*B*urn brightly without burning out.

———

RICHARD BIGGS

*H*ow far you go in life depends on
your being tender with the young,
compassionate with the aged,
sympathetic with the striving,
and tolerant with the weak...
because in your life you will
have been all of these.

———

GEORGE WASHINGTON CARVER

He who has health has hope.

And he who has hope has everything.

———

ARABIAN PROVERB

Failure is only the opportunity to begin again more intelligently.

HENRY FORD

*T*hrow your heart over the fence

and the rest will follow.

———

NORMAN VINCENT PEALE

Finish each day and be done with it.
You have done what you could; some blunders
and absurdities have crept in; forget them as soon
as you can. Tomorrow is a new day; you shall begin
it serenely and with too high a spirit to be
encumbered with your old nonsense.

RALPH WALDO EMERSON

A happy family

is but an earlier heaven.

———

GEORGE BERNARD SHAW

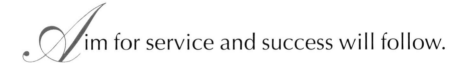

Aim for service and success will follow.

ALBERT SCHWEITZER

Wisdom is knowing

the right path to take…

integrity is taking it.

———

M.H. MCKEE

*L*ook at everything as though
you are seeing it for the first time,
with eyes of a child, fresh
with wonder.

———

JOSEPH CORNELL

Our attitude towards others determines their attitude towards us.

EARL NIGHTINGALE

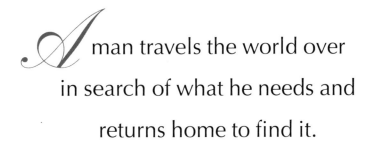

A man travels the world over
in search of what he needs and
returns home to find it.

GEORGE MOORE

*N*othing happens... but first a dream.

CARL SANDBURG

*S*elf-respect is
the fruit of discipline.

———

ABRAHAM HESCHEL

The way to gain a good reputation is to endeavor to be what you desire to appear.

———

SOCRATES

*T*he most important thing about goals is…

having one.

GEOFFRY ABERT

$\mathcal{T}$his is the beginning of a new day.

You have been given this day to use as you will.

You can waste it or use it for good.

What you do today is important because you are

exchanging a day of your life for it.

When tomorrow comes, this day will be gone forever; in its place is something that you have left behind…let it be something good.

UNKNOWN

A bird does not sing
because it has an answer.
It sings because it has a song.

———

CHINESE PROVERB

Honesty is the first chapter

in the book of wisdom.

———

THOMAS JEFFERSON

*D*on't be afraid to take a big step if needed.

You can't cross a chasm in two small jumps.

UNKNOWN

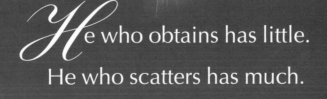

*H*e who obtains has little.

He who scatters has much.

———

LAO TZU

Kind words can be short and easy
to speak, but their echoes are
truly endless.

———

MOTHER TERESA

*L*ive your life each day as you
would climb a mountain. An occasional glance
toward the summit keeps the goal in mind,
but many beautiful scenes are to be observed
from each new vantage point. Climb slowly, steadily,
enjoying each passing moment; and the view from the
summit will serve as a fitting climax for the journey.

HAROLD V. MELCHERT

I expect to pass through life but once.
If therefore, there can be any kindness
I can show, or any good thing I can do
to any fellow being, let me do it now,
and not defer or neglect it,
as I shall not pass this way again.

WILLIAM PENN

When you get the choice to sit it out or dance…

I hope you dance…I hope you dance.

———

LEE ANN WOMACK

Success is a journey,
not a destination.

—————

BEN SWEETLAND

Wrong turns are as important as right turns.

More important sometimes.

———

RICHARD BACH

Progress involves risk.

You can't steal second base and

keep your foot on first.

———

FREDERICK WILCOX

*T*he best sermons are lived, not preached.

———

COWBOY WISDOM

*K*eep your face to the sunshine
and you will not see the shadows.

———

HELEN KELLER

The greatest risk in life is . . .

never taking one.

———

An investment in knowledge
pays the best interest.

BENJAMIN FRANKLIN

*L*aughter is an instant vacation.

MILTON BERLE

*F*ocus on the critical few…
not the insignificant many.

———

UNKNOWN

Courage is the finest of human qualities because it guarantees all the others.

WINSTON CHURCHILL

*S*itting silently beside a friend who is hurting may be the best gift we can give.

UNKNOWN

*I*t's choice – not chance –

that determines your destiny.

———
JEAN NIDETCH

What lies behind us, and what lies before us are small matters compared to what lies within us.

RALPH WALDO EMERSON

We must become the change

we want to see in the world.

———

MAHATMA GANDHI

*T*he best and most beautiful things in life

cannot be seen, not touched,

but are felt in the heart.

HELEN KELLER

*B*y being yourself, you put

something wonderful in the world

that was not there before.

———

EDWIN ELLIOT

That love is all there is
is all we know of love.

———

EMILY DICKINSON

The worst prison

would be a closed heart.

———

POPE JOHN PAUL II

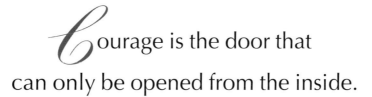

Courage is the door that

can only be opened from the inside.

TERRY NEIL

*Y*ou can't live a perfect day
without doing something for someone
who will never be able to repay you.

———

JOHN WOODEN

Watch your thoughts, for they become words.
Choose your words, for they become actions.
Understand your actions, for they become habits.
Study your habits, for they will become your character.
Develop your character, for it becomes your destiny.

————

UNKNOWN

Success is not the key to happiness.
Happiness is the key to success.
If you love what you are doing,
you will be successful.

HERMAN CAIN

Every thought is a seed.
If you plant crab apples, don't count
on harvesting Golden Delicious.

BILL MEYER

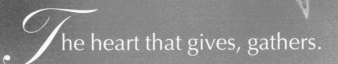

$\mathcal{T}$he heart that gives, gathers.

MARIANNE MOORE

*E*ven if you are on the right track,
you'll get run over if you
just sit there.

———

WILL ROGERS

It takes a lot of courage

to show your dreams to someone else.

ERMA BOMBECK

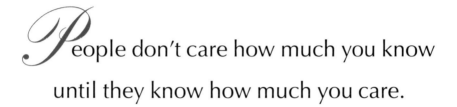

People don't care how much you know
until they know how much you care.

———

MIKE MCNIGHT

In dreams and in love

there are no impossibilities.

———

JANOS ARANY

*E*njoy the little things,
for one day you may look back and
realize they were the big things.

————

ROBERT BRAULT

The greatest power that a person possesses

is the power to choose.

J. MARTIN KOHE

*I*f there is no wind, row.

LATIN PROVERB

$\mathcal{T}$he only things that stand between a person

and what they want in life are the will to try it,

and the faith to believe it's possible.

RICH DEVOS

finding joy

A hundred years from now, it will not matter
what my bank account was, the sort of house
I lived in, or the kind of car I drove.
But the world may be different because I was
important in the life of a child.

Person to person, moment to moment, as we love, we change the world.

SAMAHRIA KAUFMAN

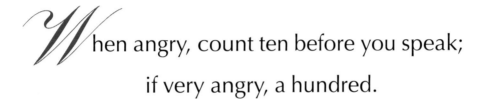

When angry, count ten before you speak;

if very angry, a hundred.

THOMAS JEFFERSON

*S*ometimes in the winds of change

we find our true direction.

The two most powerful warriors
are patience and time.

———

LEO TOLSTOY

People are about as happy

as they make up their minds to be.

———

ABRAHAM LINCOLN

Hot heads and cold hearts

never solved anything.

BILLY GRAHAM

To love and be loved

is to feel the sun from both sides.

———

DAVID VISCOTT

*L*ife begins when you do.

———

HUGH DOWNS

Love may not make the world go around,

but it sure makes the ride worthwhile.

———

FRANKLIN JONES

You cannot do a kindness too soon, for you never know how soon it will be too late.

RALPH WALDO EMERSON

*A*gainst the force of laughter

nothing can stand.

———

MARK TWAIN

$\mathcal{W}$isdom begins in wonder.

———

SOCRATES

Failure is the condiment

that gives success its flavor.

TRUMAN CAPOTE

*S*ometimes you earn more
by doing things that pay nothing.

TODD RUTHMAN

*S*ome things have to be believed
to be seen.

———

RALPH HODGSON

The heart knows, the heart knows…

listen to your heart.

———

KATHY SHERMAN

About the Author

Mac Andersonis the founder of Simple Truths and Successories, Inc., the leader in designing and marketing products for motivation and recognition. These companies, however, are not the first success stories for Mac. He was also the founder and CEO of McCord Travel, the largest travel company in the Midwest, and part owner/VP of sales and marketing for Orval Kent Food Company, the country's largest manufacturer of prepared salads.

His accomplishments in these unrelated industries provide some insight into his passion and leadership skills. He also brings the same passion to his speaking where he speaks to many corporate audiences on a variety of topics, including leadership, motivation, and team building.

Mac has authored or co-authored thirteen books that have sold over three million copies. His titles include:

- *Change is Good ... You Go First*
- *Customer Love*
- *Motivational Quotes*
- *212°: The Extra Degree*
- *The Power of Attitude*
- *The Dash*
- *Finding Joy*
- *Charging the Human Battery*
- *Learning to Dance in the Rain*
- *You Can't Send a Duck to Eagle School*
- *The Nature of Success*
- *The Essence of Leadership*
- *To a Child, Love is Spelled T-I-M-E*

For more information about Mac, *visit www.simpletruths.com*

If you have enjoyed this book we invite you to check out our entire collection of gift books, with free inspirational movies, at **www.simpletruths.com.** You'll discover it's a great way to inspire *friends* and *family,* or to thank your best *customers* and *employees.*

Our products are **not available in bookstores ... only direct.** Therefore, when you purchase a gift from Simple Truths you're giving something that can't be found elsewhere!

For more information, please visit us at:
www.simpletruths.com Or call us toll free… **800-900-3427**